STEPS

Other books by Maurice Scully:

STEPS

Maurice Scully

REALITY STREET EDITIONS
1998

Published by
REALITY STREET EDITIONS
4 Howard Court, Peckham Rye, London SE15 3PH
and
6 Benhall Green, Saxmundham, Suffolk IP17 1HU

acknowledgements: *versions of some of these pieces appeared in
pamphlet form as* Certain Pages *from* Form Books, *London and*
Over & Through, *Poetical Histories, Cambridge. Other parts
appeared in* Active in Airtime, Angel Exhaust, Exact Change
Yearbook, Fire, Shearsman *and* World Letter.

STEPS *is vol 4 of* LIVELIHOOD, The Set, *a work in 5 books
(1986-1997).*

Typesetting by Ken Edwards

Printed & bound in Great Britain
by Antony Rowe Ltd, Chippenham

A catalogue record for this book is available from the British
Library

ISBN: 1-874400-15-6

Eastern Arts
Board Funded

... agus a haon, dó, trí

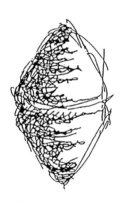

STEPS

To go in one machine on the road watching
another machine in the sky. To enter the
machine I'm travelling in I entered a card
in a machine going a progress through the
suburbs where all the houses are the same.
Lock hands and hope, let the mood deepen,
step into/down to learn, to change machines.
The one in the sky has entered cloud and
disappears. But the sound ...

I see a globe wrapped up in occupied flight-
paths on a screen. I hear the light noise of
the buttons on the keyboard depressed. The
ravine between you and the world you're supposed
to be in wasn't a dream, and. Turn. Passing
an insect on a wall, its supple antennae already
measuring (Time = Energy - Money x Hope).
What have we missed? Who is reporting what
to whom? Turn sharply into the less well-known.

This? A high-pitched melody from the digital watch
on your wrist in the desert. Which type of hype is
the best type, the most manipulative, the most
lie-laden? Gecko, stopped. Beat, pluck, tickle
the rhythm through! A tiny cloud, one bright wisp,
to the west moves — in time, burin nicks — moves
just a little bit, moves me, *ah*.

RETICLE

Move in: the web shivers (my father
swimming in the open sea, those strong,
unmistakeable strokes, link to link) a
dust of scales, greenish purple, towards
the thorax on the bramble stem, edged,
programmed trap, and your fingers
tingle. Take time as a solid. I was alive in
and overhearing what? Step.

Suddenly this morning on the way to the shop
in the blackthorn bush by the railway track
I picked out a birdcall I'd never before heard.
So. Or this afternoon coming back from the
post office the clean whorl of a snail's shell
on a white wall. Stopped. And stopped again,
thanks, to take in five more such on a
gable-end, each different, streaked, polished,
echo-ported, glazing a trail to nowhere
in particular just then.

Open your books, checking the bunched items in
the seam, yes, but skirt the piranha pool, the trick
of engagement in the air, thick. Look. Applause and
photographs. Where will the filament fall? What small
breeze take our lives away? I dip my hand in. *Spang*
goes the Giant's buckle, again.

IN THE MUSIC

When the leaves wither and begin to blaze and
fall all the way down the ladder to each
rootweb's radius in a plot they make a brittle
miracle of beginning a paintbox on the bright grass,
the die set. There it is, in the slack between
one of the little stopped waves on the tin roof
over where I know its nest is in under the beam
over the window, flea-hunting. Quick–quick, gone.
Log: at the Problem Wall at the heart of the maze,
do not impose your will.

Being all ambiguous cloud-places and so quiet so/
that *is* there could be thought to/I think they/
what's that? trickle on the map, a musaic, (could
be an omen, I mean, amen), cloudberry and hare's-tail
cotton grass, "messages come in flashes," ready or
not. Nonetheless. Perhaps. However. Argument.
Disputation. Dichotomy. All circles, glints that in
the cross-grain/skarns/revert; do not impose your will.

Is it really the 10th? Can't be. Wait a minute. (So
many facts, so much manufacture, so little prey).
Tipply-pip, says the bird, *do-you-agree, do-you-agree.*
Sometimes, briefly, even here I/or/I do. But then ...
A cat in the grass, amity, seedcup.

SONNET

In it build. A wall of tiny, precise, bricks,
a wall of fittings, of feelings, discoveries,
evasive shadows, a wall of absence collected,
wall of tears justified, the wall of plain
speaking. If the system locks you to the screen
it directs your life. Leave the room. Breathe
in. The wall moves out a bit. Blue pen, red pen,
the many ways through: put that in your pocket
to feel better in times of distress ... yes?

An old wine bottle base found in a wall
built a century ago around a house in rural Ireland
now in a case in a museum in a castle in the middle
of Ireland under my odd pink reflection
peering up; with what intention? Click. Sunlight
on a chimney pot. A crow on a roof. Shocked by
the shards that fly past my face here: a "career in
'development'," the "management of the poor." And
lodge in the receptive surface of the wall opposite
and disappear.

MARCHING SONG

Tittle on the drum. A seated figure
at a desk from the back. A ten shun.
A tube of dust. Descending steps. In
sum. It's. It's the way they're always
"they" and never ever ever. Ever.

Plant your feet on the ground as the
basis evaporates in a blur of academic
backchat/I think I/Got that? Turn round.
As if as if as if ... The point of the
story, the point of all his little stories
was, note, *poor me.*

•

As if the running could ever stop anyway,
each sour step collecting bitterness at each
failure to pause to close the spaces between
things and their settings, selfish, lazy, blind,
deaf, never growing up, never wanting to,
even their own children sacrificed to
particularly their own children sacrificed to
this ego-dark, this maw. Is the point.
How do you feel about that? Close the book.

Daystar on a branchtip, raindrop holding in.
They'll come, they'll succour and lay siege,
furtive and uninvited in the early hours,
vanishing in a cloud of ionized futures busy
under the sun beginning. Dry sticks, foot-
prints in the dust.   /...

•

(A) Walk away, and their weapons are gone;
laugh at yourself (B) and they bury themselves
in their own muck. Let everything, as it
happens, (C) happen between brackets, and the
brackets (dreaming) bulge, skip, loop.

The sun *block* the moon; the night *block* the day;
winter-spring-summer *block* the autumn top; tap trowel,
scrape. The gap between the footsteps on the stoep.

PARTS

slate a blueback stone
"black stone"

chalk a white stone
"chalk"

learning to follow
the way you hear the talk

you will learn to follow
the ways you see the talk
deployed

& learn to initiate deployments
in surprise
measuring surprise
crestfallen by the word *is*

& this habit
will facilitate & hinder
yr ideas about the world
skintight   to itself

in the darkness
(&) in the light.

•

/...

to speak in the foreground

fateful relation

to speak in the foreground

not by
    addition
    subtraction

to keep the light ground cored

as the conditions amass

as the fate is set

budbursts in the light
as against mass murder

to eke out what the ore can tell

of the dew of heaven
& the fatness of the earth

before the end

to speak in the foreground

shiver of calculation

    dark.light

•

/...

the tune of tact
(as you write)
the skill of gifting well
(as you speak)
an appropriate pacing

facing the proper way
(in the light).

no dearth of boxes
shiny tight spacious
(ice rosettes where the ice is cut
dice caught falling to earth heard knock)
yr life locked in at the edges.

for how long do you plan to
carry *that* contradiction?

•

(2 hands to yr cheeks re-
calling. kiss.

pretty head in the crowd
more alive than
any old petal on a bough.
goodbye).

•

from stone
lichen
on clear air, coaxed.

17

IN THE MUSIC

There is a ball, a sphere. There is a field,
a rectangle. At each end a space, an Aperture.
Markings on the field and men, marked and
numbered. A set of rules, a set time, a whistle,
an umpire, an audience. The phantasy of pride of
skill in tactical symmetry, the siphon of violent
energies, the bonding of comrades, place-adoration,
display-therapy: our gift, your tradition! A poet
under the grassblades, threnody in the palmtrees.
There is a ball, a sphere.

Giving back a black mesh, all the rules together, connected,
or if all the rules together, dilated, make a path out then/
Then the rules get up and shake hands. Game, set. No

I mean yes. Turn. Tangled up in its geometry the tree
sprouts TREE (in English, but not in Italy). *Chak*. (*Again*
is the sequent matgic). If, stepping inside around and then
outside and then again inside the circle of the rules of
the game is the game, what then? Got that? *Chak*. But that's
a new game. Turn, dance. Busy, busy, busy

SONNET
the words

They are building a house, note
and accrete, tat-tat. On the map.
That. I. But. Building a place
on a place so that/is yr cell
in the hive quite adequate? Patches
of leaf. Conduit, shadow. Walling
and windowing, dooring and flooring,
a wandering idiot, humming and
hawing, hello-ing and no-ing, oh
yes. The shimmer of advancing futures,
the oily consecutive links, building
a dream on a fact.

Cut down. Lieing in bed, lying in
bed. Games in the laneway — Pluck-&-
Recant, Dip-it-in-Blood — keeping the
smooth hollow of the blowpipe clean,
lap and accrete tat-tat. Building a
house in the air. Then the air moved aside
to the music. And the music come round
wrapped in that. Cut down. Or didn't you
hear? Braided Tunnels, Places-You've-Been-To,
Pivots, Webs, Crystals shiver to the cliff's
edge and over, and then, (just that), and then
learning, dolce, you can fly, dolce, then.
All praise.

But, to recap: a house, a shed, a shield, a tree,
its shadow, appalled, collapsed, afloat, aloof,
amen. Amen, tat-tat. Amen tat-tat. Afloat, aloof,
amen.

IN PRAISE OF PAINTING DOORS
for Louis' recovery

If your five-year-old son falls from a high wall
to concrete and fractures his skull, concentrate
your love. Focus everything. Everything. Everything,
day and night. Everything.

Afterwards, all going well, leaving the hospital,
take brushes and white spirit. Everything. Don't
underestimate the virtù of the clean rag in the pocket.

White can be a bore, that's true.

On the other hand, a whole lifetime can be a foil (too).

That the conference/congruence of colours in the world
has something to do with the pulsebeat of blood in the
human body might be worth looking into. But not yet.
Hell! *Rag*.

At waist level, sit and paint to your patient boot-top.
The spine deserves pleasure too, not panic, not despair.

Don't be proud of your house. Obviously … The jackal
solicitor has his fangs in your neck. And there's the
little matter of deep time. Paint on.

Walls speak to doors. Doors answer back. However much
tempted, never intrude.

/...

In the hallway. In the living-room. Oh, and here's one:
"in the 'utility room'." Now where do I live?

My children's feet in their shoes on the floor.

Fly with the positive possible energies landing only
to watch in delight.

You too were something once.

Return brushes to spirit. A force in the body of the work
demands it. Sit, eat. Ashtree sapling outside in the play-
breeze by the window.

Having shed clutter, to the next house go, with a light
pocket, a light heart, a light touch, a fire in the mind,
and a plan, lightly carried, as lightly let go.

STEPS

He is moving a ladder. He is climbing it.
He is whistling. The sound of a jet. The
sound of someone sawing wood. A cat moves
smoothly along (hammertap of hands fixing tiles
to slats) the granite coping of the cottage
in the laneway. Stops. Disappears over the
rooftop.

Downwind of your nightsky time-probing telescope's
definitely not apples, or clove oil or myrrh!
Chipped granitic plug. Pad along past the lip
of the last grip, let fly ...

You'd slept well and rose immediately,
kettle on, bundle of papers out to the shed
at the end of the garden through the dewy grass.
In detail and proliferation (hoverfly's
pulsing abdomen, secret nectary opened out)
a ladybird beetle ambling past through
the proliferate grass. Is that the word for it?
A woodlouse dropped off the door-jamb, so quiet you
could hear it drop.

SOUND

What cruder machine than the machine
you think can listen. The machines get
up and dance, sit down and cry. So it
seems. The withdrawal of information,
distortions, ludicrous non-choices among the
snapping fangs. What's this nonsense about
voting? Wake up. Or "Why do men fish
when they're not hungry?"   (Leda, 6).

Just before dawn you can think straight.
A good fit, as it happens, apt; bigger vistas,
less credulity. A lifetime in segments
up to that point. Then start again.
A gain. Pliancy. On the other hand ...

Sound of the flame flicker, sound of your
scratching your head, listening in. From
the outside of your life, a pattern threaded
through, to the inside of your life, what at
the back of your mind coming to the front,
tautens. Look, I move my fingers. Oh. Feeling
the pull of that nearby star the river twists
and spins. Then I began to walk about with
my body again.

SONNET

1: Move in: shiver. It rises with the strange
crisis of the heat and the blazing moon
in the dark. This is not a conversation with
anything like anything you could like. I
know I know I know the muffled tape downstairs,
practiced blues. Living in tiers. Worry about
worry in a package won't get your eyes
off the microfiche zipping by in a blur.

2: Climbed Kholo Mountain one misty Sunday morning
at a time of year when the initiation schools
were not in session. Herdboys with sticks,
Basotho blankets, outsized rubber boots,
scampered up and down the slopes and sang
initiation songs in the caves. We came to the lake
and they gathered kindling for us. Gossip. Gossip,
just under the surface, edging in, through, involving
itself in the flow, sticking its ego-clamp over
the plan, gossiping, gossiping ... *Vide cor tuum*.

3: This is the stark shaft of moonlight, the one tree
for miles in the dark, on the plain, its shadow, struck.
Durability, scrupulousness and the record; these, are
the three things.

STEPS
the tune

It impinges to such a degree that the minimum
function required to remain the anonymous
human agent in the world exerts a pressure
disproportionate to the results required. *Chiaro?*
Birdsong. I am the perfect citizen. Nothing is
nothing. Yes-ing and no-ing and on-the-other-hand-
ing my way through the mesh. I mean mess. Just
pre-set the dial for Discipline: palm-frond in
Harare, a bridge in Cambridge shiver a synapse.

•

adze-cut coral rag
(2 block sizes)
lilac spike/key on a string.
the first floret
you ever looked into
termite tunnels
mimosa flicker

(coming to
coming through
coming round)

filaments in a ring.

FIRE

Moving through the shadows under the trees,
diamonds and islands of light sliding over
the figure disappearing into the dark,
the closely-felted interlocking needle-like
crystals of feldspar with a scattering of
colourful smaller crystals of olivine
and pyroxene and some black specks of
iron oxide/then one. Sharp. Jab. Move,
if you dare. Before you start anything,
stop.

The magic mice make gold. The beautiful
poor girl's hair is gold. The boulder rolls
from the cave's mouth disclosing gold.
Gold, gold. There is gold leaf to each tree
and a rich vein under the forest imminent.
Then I woke up.

Rest your head in your hand. Task: (still)
fill in the spaces between the waves of
that echo. Draw close. Opal. The mango fills
your palm and weights it, scrupulous, before
you bargain, before you speak, before you
breathe again, calm.

IN THE MUSIC

•••

The route turns sharply under the railway track, then
turns again, sharply, up. Look back at the town, the other
way. Sit on the limestone drywall. A dog goes by. (*Will* is
the tense where the problem is)./I turn out of my way to
take in the laneway to the side of the park to visit the
sycamore and goose grass, cuckoo spit, placing my foot
beside a pool of what sky it catches and touch (travelling)
limestone wallblocks, lichen rosettes, that small group to
the right of venerable pine, lime and chestnut further on,
oh yes, by the court-house. Smile to myself. The fossil
record. (Only *will* is the tense where the problem is)./The
light come a long way to play in all these busy, invisible
canals goes back — *ah* — memory as an agglutinative
wobble of soundwaves? Some time passed

& then
suddenly we heard again the same deep trumpet-like sound
we'd heard from a distance when we entered the lagoon.

Then a dozen or so men came forward, went into the hut,
they were playing strange trumpets and flutes,
breathless now, breathless
with emotion &
delight.

•••

RESPONSIBILITY

the fid; stirps.

not to write very cold poetry.

that events of social/political significance
be *witnessed* seemed reasonable enough & yet.

ha! pro deo pro patria & the tightening knot
at the top of the spine.

long lines of characteristic compact crowns
suckering vigorously in hedgerows.

they've never had children.

there it is, yr ache, fibrous, gripping the
secret verbum at the basis: *take, take, take,*
kerfed & set into the rabbets.

little nude screams.

coda

in the tree's underchamber
the roots enmesh & thicken

(I know   I know   I know)

after white silence
the yellow growthsound

very   quite
delicate   listen

FIRE

low sky
gull   aerial
head that way
this
beak wide
calls
        snowthroat
        snowpulse
calls
        then

a crow's
outer wing
upturned
on the
downthrust
in the upwind
the dancer
stepped through
the laneway
one–two

two–five
before you looked
out the little
window
down the
street   /...

in snow
(speck that
you are,
babyfist)
pod
oh
glyph-continuing
trackfollowing
one male adult
the wind blew
I could tell
this way not

that when/vast
dustmass incub
ating stars/
smell of
catpiss or
what's–it
flowering
currant?
(pod)
& a dog got
about too
quite busy
in its
early morning
check–around.

/...

two shadows
a third
grey ply
black/red
dix-huit
dix-huit
wingflash
wingbeat
well &
good.

low sky.

•••

a cup of water on the table
the table on the floor
the floor on the ceiling
of the next cell down

the drizzle continues & then
continues a fine web
revealing fine webs shimmering over
the table shivering five crumbs of bread

shimmering or prove it otherwise
organized spaces so that
definitely everything we did say
we read we hadn't did they said now.

MATURITY

The smell of cypress in the summer, that grey
roof among the trees picked out by the sun
on the side of a small hill in the distance;
young, in through the eyes, the strong tang
of the world impacting its *itself* on you, a
tide of smallest, simplest things.

The big idea was God. When it first entered
the language meaning *Loud Noise*/but don't let's
get/And a century or two of that kept them
happy. Or quiescent. Or moral. Or stupid. Or
blocked up. One day in the summer of '52; then —
lilac tree in flower — today. Is it raining?

Nothing is nothing. I am the perfect citizen.
Finitude is rubbish, everybody knows that.
No wonder the secret police are busy. Phone me
(to lie in bed Understanding Poetry) phone me
when you get back.

FOUR CORNERS

The language spits pidgin dominance

And from a height.

•

A curious parallel with

Birdsong.

□□□

PERMISSION

who, diabetic, prone to gangrene, lost both
legs   bit by bit

whose family abandoned him to the hospital

whose wife realigned

whose case was taken up

who arrived back suddenly from the hospital
in a wheelbarrow

who was constrained to sleep separately

whose gable collapsed in the rainy season but
seemed nonetheless content to live thus till
his son came back from the mines   a tidy
compound & a hard wife

who employed himself with us one day out of the
blue under a tree cutting the branches he could
reach for kindling for tobacco money & just never
afterwards quite went away

who got about with chunks of tyres on his stumps

who never missed a party at our place

who must have watched me sit my young daughter
on the slowly disappearing wooden fence of our compound
(quality firewood) of an evening for a chat

/...

whose son came back from the mines in the end &, drunk,
thanked us   florid & a little, somehow, threatening

•

so.

that Threads can intersect at the dead mesh of

Poignancy (yellow dust at my feet, blue
mountains, far sky)(I am quite sensible
to this) if let.

& yet.   so.

RESPONSIBILITY

Washing her clothes in a rusty
old wheelbarrow by the dam by the
track under the eucalyptus where
the frogs at night fill the vill-
age air with/her bright brown eyes
and mouth connect in a smile whose
radiance and playfulness the fine
skin black/I thought I could get to
know almost everything once not quite
yet feeling the bounce in the net
(The Oxford English Dictionary of
Spraints, The Pretoria Encyclopaedia
of Mortgages, The Concise Cambridge
Political), when arcane thinking
clicks in its conduit. Tap: "an artist
is *never* poor." Swallow that.

BALLAD

the dance of the world in the world is the world
an old steel pump, Victorian, at the foot of a dune
which still gives water   still

•

marram builds   directed   builds
my children too [learn, learn, learn & do]
& that most pliant of materials: questions-&-execrations.

•

under the sycamore, plants on the wall, a fly dipping
its head into nectar, sources swaying, shimmering,
the systems, the structures melt & swell reflected upside-
down in the bubble in the skull going by. link to link
      smile. the piercing yelp of the frustrated infant.

•

wood being fine, too, link, super-fine, following the
denier, the grain, gave me leave to love at last, link,
in the blue sky after rain birdsong to seem more clear
at last: the first small spider in the new house
its shadow, moving   dot   each plan plain. procumbent.
it would seem.

•

response: *look* — the whorled grooves of the seed-pellets,
meadowsweet.

•

... plant them.

RAIN

then cut the wood   with care   following the line
ply & tooth   the weapons are nothing   mind yr hand
keep time   cutting true & crude   then

tacked it   silver through yellow   a whole mountainside on fire

webshadow/masterstrand affix, set by, scoop & try shedding what
(little insect on the page) writing writhing riding
the waves' more basic music trebled, trembled   allows

& dreamtracing (the weapons are nothing) the array   a
light in the language   a light for the language
alighted in the dust of a hilltop village   the weapons   which

                    is the flower you
                    can grip this flower with
                    extreme care

                    once   are nothing

                    clicks & ululations ...

the smoky homework of my students

the hopeful homework of my students

the struggle in the homework of my students

                                        /...

the pathos in correcting the sad, smoky homework
of my students

.ı. big, braided rivers.

STEPS

a

driving in a red dustcloud
for hours years wandering
wondering how to

connect

this stone to that hut with
precision tact   two hands one
gift   wait listen   right
left   shimmering elastic

wallhome
(not any other barrier
but a breeze over it)
welcoming.   conduit.

b

blue flower   strong stem
oval stone in the stream

I was stepping lightly home
(the baby developing)

starlings' jabber-click
cutting with the burin nick

/...

conical hills   stone outcrop
two swans   one rooftop

dead flower   dead stem
dead stone in the stream

a fish shadows by. a cloud.
a bird. wake up, coward.

c

window lit
fire in the grate
door closed over
table set

the food being ready
ready the appetite
(in dreams begin steadi-
ness) come, sit —

peeling a piece
of bark to get
the smell of
the tree feeding —

when threads mesh as they cross
over they sing to us.

this is how to live.

AISLING

salt
in the sand &
a sand–

stone
boulder standing
beside a

sand–
dune where the
marram

points
the way the wind
went

strong
long in the wind where
(closer)

shadows
skim, touch, cut
into

deeper
dark in which dark
Darkness

darkened ...
hollows, pockets, echoes,
what

/...

Perfect
is & *Rightness* &
Justice

(a
Giant turning in his
skin)

but
nothing accommodates
it, nothing

a game
of rule-changing,
finding

the fulcrum
enveloping slate &
brick

leaf &
bark & a broken tin, breathe
in, this too,

out, slit,
flower of surprising shocks,
growth-rings,

code messages,
strange processes in secret
underground

a flower
locked(in secret)underground
but   /...

feeling
the pull of that nearby star ...
this

vertical
pinprick pipsqueak —
Perception!

(possible
states & possible
combinations)

each
a gift a
burden

each —
prophecy, friendship,
finitude

wrapped
up in foolishness &
yearning —

seven
apertures, one
head.

RETICLE

The feel of the twigs in your
hands dry, dead, aromatic, the
passingness of/but the sides of the song
brush the fire in it and kindle/slap
goes the foot in the wet/slap/where
was I?/the/slap/tempo to honour the/
then rain/slap/fire/busy in the
world/slap/. A tripod in a bubble!
Slashed and bitten; clawed, hacked,
chopped. Tightened in the bud,
talisman, not an arrow telling
a narrow story, but/stamp/dash, splash
and/sound of the money in the building
in the undergrowth/display. What?

•

A rat attracted by the wheat in the
poison in the attic fell dead one
night behind where I sat. I was fin-
ishing a book; gathering kindling;
sleeping in the loft beside a glass-
covered gap in the gable, the window.
Politics. Afforested drumlin, ghost-
mist in the outwash.

This world is different, that one the
same. Patiently to disclose how little
you know, the crow-echo in the chimney
flue, the pet cricket. Step.   /...

•

Cloudwisps connect. Correct. Crystals
lock the seed in. Correct. The smell of
nettles, water, watermint, willowsilver
in the air by the stream in the breeze,
clay, crushed grass–music, these take you
about and turn about together in the dreampool.
Correct. Flick and dazzle, the freedom to
move, step, the colours at the base, on site,
prior, primary, jigdance, write: fire

FIRE

fire
a quick breeze among
the leaves pushes the
music lightly
into the visible &
through it out again
gone. forsythia begins:
a bright sudden *thanks*.
    here. (hand)   then
    up   there   (wing)
    en   closed.
knows a
way. away
over
there.
over.
    in a flicker of
    stabs at the vast
    central column of
    (   )(being)
    (contacting zig-zag
    connecting verticals)
    (the air in the bones
    of the bird in flight)
    a miraculous access
    twists: once. &
    once. calling
    to each other in
    hedges & trees.
what's in the news then?   /...

the water in the river
in the circle at that point,
political. dark cell
old things
flat on your back
stone on the belly.
    imprint in the mud
    on the bank.
predawn whimper of the pump
in the dust.

FOUR CORNERS

PASTORAL
Skin of the earth on the
earth   the fragility

agility
profusion of bud–plans

of   &
blot   manoeuvre   corrode

do I/we/you/they
have to repeat even more
more?

It's
PASTORAL
When grasslands disappear
& the slopes are denuded

the topsoil
without grip

... the finial pit
of the first recorded

raindrop

bangs
the tympanum.

/...

Let
PASTORAL

Small wave-like motion of
sound/someone singing

in a radio in a
kitchen over a

hedge on a windowledge
somewhere not far off.

Some bits
of words of
interest

or is it a
woman singing

outside the radio
her heart out?
PASTORAL

Valleys, villages, coastline. The map
of the stain on the wall. Alive & living,
not a crammed glasshouse of pistillate
verba. The grass bends back. The book
is fat, contains code. The world,
the water planet. The code contained in
this thing in the world, the book, changes
the things, the world. The elytral suture
opens & the wings, surprising & beautiful,
begin to work. The point is. Fernbrush,
nervure of such wings, small pebble
adjustments. Song.

55

IN THE MUSIC

Who's minting the tickets anyway?
I mean, looking back, an orchestral These-Which is what
    presents in the filter, yes?

Philosophy: tell me, is there a hole in the future?
Tell me, who sticks Advice to the webs?
Wait, I said (Choreography) wait a minute (delicate
    interconnected communities) is yr head yr home, the
    world a vigorous perianth of seven hundred billion
    teeth?

Tacit slap of underwater wave-fold, secret sub-shadows
    taking in the beat of the solar roar in yr ear where
    xenophilia built a commentary, the clouded leopard,
    bramble and grasses, smell of the green laneway in
    the summer rain, a fly hitting a windowpane. Click.
I let's see ah yes.

CODA

RAIN

when I look at what's
I wonder dust between
the toes just branches
that don't catch/what
underlies what? a wrong
tack that but/stone leaf
air give back fumbling
along a path almost some-
times to con even yr
even yrself
talk to yr children
eye to eye
talk to yr children
not embargoes &
economic sanctions talk
to yr children wait
for what impact comes
from such (instar) such/
matted & black/fernhead,
nutrient moisture at
the grasstip the more
the most complete
stupidity globed. so. &
returns. sprung vertical
from the bud discutient
properties in gravel &
knots in the body
my little boy's first
tooth to go is so
small & perfect   /...

ly tapered & white

there's birdsong & light
mint underfoot   sums.

spoon, chalk, cup. the empty
pocket & the raindrop.
down between ply, counterply
almost every edge's argument
holds. (or do they?)
(seafóideach!)★ jostle & equate.
big pencil in childfist.
that. just that.

★Irish: silly, nonsense

RETICLE

A

Years ago one winter evening travelling
through Ireland on a bus I watched the
moon like money in the sky. (I dislike
similes, Mary, you know me). The moon
was like money. Like money. Pulsing in
the breast-pocket, bright sterile dust-
rock, just like money. Circular shine
against black, a brilliant silver, crystals,
poison. The fine spray of chemicals in the
brain, that tree, this lake. The colours
on the flag ripple the wind still, that
dazzling spinning blue sphere in the dark.

Cold tonight. Paid the rent. Maybe a glint
from a passing car, a tempo gathering through
your life to here, and right to this point,
up to this point, still, still not for sale.
Provided that.

Your number please. Furry pod. Living in a
dream of news where information magnified to
a grainy blur ... Made a few things, maybe a
few things, thought-gathering. At least the
pedant busy with his pedantry, but here
an ache of disciplined listenings over long
spaces, to make "a this" that is not for sale.

/...

B

That box, that lamp, that bottle on the table.
You follow the path, eyes down, ears beginning —
the pursuit of healing — intricate alleyways
in crushed grass fibre under a stone,
bright ant-eggs, at least this pedant busy
with his pedantry, but here ... the music.
Clocks. A thousand buried years of not opening up
until something — heat and shock — oozes through.

C

Talking colours with my son — he's five, I'm
thirty-nine/he's right, I'm an idiot — the wren,
arrowtailed shadow in the hedgeplace, ready, each
crease in the hawthorn's argument, the leaves move.
Catch your foot in a hollow. Tap on the drum.

Tip scales: black sky, then rain. Flashes.
And this rain hammers out a drama on the ground
sending up steam and a loud roar on the tin roof
and a shiver up the spine. And someone is ringing
a bell in the village to hurry this angry spirit
on. Move on, move on. Kindle, kindling, kind, kin,
kine, K, the yellow, the red earth washing into
the dongas and away.

STEPS

wake dreaming I mean you can
    wake up dreaming
or dream living; what's that?
    branch-tap.

bell rings, on the wind,
    & wavers & rings.
a table & a Table-
    Waiting-for-Things

through the chorus moving
    the song along to/but
not for long, not for longing.
    feet on the ground

    yr feet on the ground
    out of the

        blue.

FIRE

A

suddenness of what snow does
to a doorstep when you
wake to it in the morning
early before almost anyone

(& why the verb *to be*
in so many languages
at such an angle should be
so irregular so often)

a slate gone there
emphatic & there too
yes the wind blew this way
not that when

(is a mystery to me.
where were you when they
named the name of money
in your name anyway?)

the snow fell graphic many
ways across you (curls joinctures
loops stops) to make the black & white
unmelting music of what is

•

/...

B

being coiled into a deft, modified past
not in money-work but secret
difficulties darkness pleated
dovetailing deeper dark down to
an all-dimensional ground blackness
being coiled into a deft, modified past
hollowing, carving, cutting (I went out.
I met nobody/I came back. Faced it.)
the greedkeep, health, sanity, calmness where
the roots are, coiled, magnified,
crystal spindles at the branch-heads,
spasm of light

        a wind that
        turns a leaf on
        the ground or
        ientate
        yourself.

        -

        grey black
        stone ochre.
        grey black
        ochre clay.

          •

some monumental crap about gathering honey
in the tympanum of a bank's facade   /...

small waterplanet tubby patriots
the minim of "known" history vertical siphon, pip.
dogfish upriver, another world
light through glass touching the light
curtain reflected on the tabletop surface
upside-down repelled
returns —
pax! paxpax! pax!
goes the fighting in the street
being coiled into a deft, modified past.

–

      grey black
      ochre stone
      grey black
      ochre clay

•

C

a triangle of sun
light on the
wall of a
shed.
      blue sky. join the
      dots. child-wit.
      the blue plane.
      the blue
      plane
draws the eye   /...

along then
down to
chim
         neys & rooftops. here
         we are. slightly
         closer to the
         heart of
creation (but still
not close enough)
at the base of
an old tree
(minute
         grains of white quartz
         imprint of the nail
         in the mud/webb-
         ing between
         3 toes
& mare's tail sprung from the ooze
a spider web, ready) a small
bird buried. even that.
the tune complifact
scraptured.
         five seagulls in V-form-
         ation & a quick
         sparrow too
         makin a
         mane.

         it's wonderful to wake up sometimes
         to the feeling of time in the morning
         early, crisp, moving for a moment in
         the first day always, the clasp & bars   /...

of the metal gate in the hedge outside
(say) by the pathway where — can do on
contact — the garden — you are — a glass
of cool water on the sunlit sill — in-
tricate tickle on the face — bright berry —
the air puckered where the silkseed
drifts *that*

held to the Waiting Posture, *that* music an instant
fit to stave only an order in a sea of which/&
orders. when a token's taken & returned
fluent — "beautiful ideas for prov-
iding truth" — a *legal-decision-*
trial-peace pouch in waiting
(pat)

clé deas
            you could ex-
    plain
                            Peru
    release the Trees
        Animals
                        Engines
    joining the
        Geometric Dance
    on the shed wall
                        of an evening
        vertical to the *why* in yr pockets
        (otherwise empty you go about with
            proud & prim nonetheless)
        mirrors gaps branch-formations
            the very sight in the head —   /...

conical hills
stone outcrops —
staving off all aggressive parasites
& ear to the beat of breathing
returned renewed & singing
why
/whirring pipsqueak/can't-thinking
why can't thinking
fit thinking fit
this apt
black black
grey red
black red
grey grey
black

•

i.m.: Paul Klee

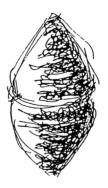

NOTE: The epigraph in Irish means & *one, two, three* a phrase commonly used to count out the steps in Irish dancing lessons.

Frontispiece/backpiece represents a clay pouch from which the Sumerian logograph ⬦ is derived, meaning, or thought to mean, *legal, decision, trial* or *peace*.

Reality Street Editions depends for its continuing existence on grants from funding bodies, sales and subscriptions, and donations from the following Supporters:

Robert Hampson
Romana Huk
Tony Lopez
Drew Milne
Ian Robinson
Spanner/Allen Fisher
Andrew Toovey
2 x anonymous

If you would like further information about subscriptions, or would like to become a Supporter of Reality Street Editions, please write to the London address on the reverse of the title page, or email
kenedwards1@compuserve.com

Web site: www.demon.co.uk/eastfield/reality/